Introduction

Introduction

I have always lived very near the seaside and to be honest, I couldn't contemplate buying and living in a home unless it had a sea view, or very close to the sea. I might make an exception for a golf course view. Still, my dream has always been to retire to a home with a picture window overlooking the ocean, preferably a large bay window with a comfy armchair, where I can sit and watch the passing traffic on the sea when I am no longer able to get out.

I have bought, renovated and lived in several old fisherman's cottages over the years, and they are not your typical home. They have some unique perspectives, quaint pleasurable aspects, and some frustrating challenges. I do not think we need to tell you about the pleasures of living in a fisherman's cottage, but we aim to cover the challenges you will face when buying a seaside retreat and what to look out for when purchasing.

Your work is merely beginning once you purchase. Although thoroughly enjoyable to sit and watch the waters' activities, a fisherman's cottage will require constant attention and repair to keep it in perfect condition. We will tell you about the most important tasks you must keep on top of, the best time to do them and the best products to use.

Finally, you will need a few tips on living in a close, tight community. Many of the homes are almost on top of each other, sometimes with shared facilities. There are legal positions to consider. More importantly, there will be local knowledge and established, unspoken and unwritten rules and pecking orders that you would do well to tip-toe your way around until you learn the lie of the land.

If you dream of living in a fisherman's cottage, looking out to sea from the comfort of your armchair at the sizeable picturesque window, then this book is a must for you before you even start looking for your property.

CHAPTER 1

Location, location, location

Chapter 1Location, location, location

Where do you start? There are millions of options and millions of answers, none of which are right or wrong. The location is simply something you need to figure out for yourself. However, we can give you some help and prodding in the right direction.

The location to buy a cottage is the first central question that needs answering and will depend on the answers to many different more minor questions you must ask yourself.

What type of location? A big city, a small village or somewhere in between? Significant city locations have better infrastructure and transport links but are not everybody's cup of tea for a relaxing holiday or retirement. What is your purpose for buying? What are you looking for in a location? Then, of course, you must consider, you don't get a whole lot of fisherman's cottages in cities, so I'm guessing most readers, considering buying a fisherman's cottage is looking for the tranquillity of a quaint village or town.

How far from your current location should you buy? Once again, this will depend on your requirements. If you are looking to retire there

BUYING AND MAINTAINING A FISHERMANS COTTAGE

BUYING AND MAINTAINING A FISHERMANS COTTAGE

JAMES WHITELAW

Swackie Ltd

CONTENTS

and have no pressing need to regularly travel back to your current lo-cation, it could be anywhere that takes your fancy. However, if you are looking to use it for short weekend getaways, you need to be looking somewhere within a reasonable driving distance.

When will you be using it? This point may seem irrelevant to you if you live in a big city. Still, you must be aware that some of these smaller villages, although idyllic in the summer, can be bleak and barren in the winter and often inaccessible. I have lived in small communities which may be completely cut off for up to a week in the winter snows. Consider whether this would be a problem for you.

How will you get there? If you are travelling by private car, you have very few restrictions. On the other hand, if you rely on public transport, some small hamlets have little or no public bus service. You will be buy-ing for the long term, so consider how your needs may change over the years. If you get a little older and are no longer able to drive, how would this affect you?

What is your budget? Fortunately, many small villages are unspoilt because there is little industry there. This also means that there is scant demand for properties, and you can pick up a real bargain. However, trendy and scenic places are often more expensive, so you must consider it too.

Do you need an income from the property? If you need or even only would prefer a return from the property, then there are many other things to consider. All the above questions need to be asked again and this time from a potential tenant's point of view.

If renting the property out, you must check if there are any restric-tions on doing this. Many municipalities categorise areas or buildings as available for short-term rental or long-term rental, with heavy penalties for non-conformance. Restrictions are seldom a problem in the UK, but many other countries may have limitations in place, building by building or even by area.

You need to check if there is someone available nearby to keep an eye on the property and carry out any emergency repairs when tenants are in place. You will also need a competent person to clean the home thoroughly after every guest.

Compare how different areas rate for local authority property charges. These can be significant between various authorities and massive between countries. A cottage in Scotland can set you back £1,000 per year, whereas a similar property in Spain would be around €200 per year.

Finally, how is the general weather pattern in your chosen area? In Scotland, where I live, the east coast is much dryer than the west coast, but the west coast has, by far, better scenery. Only you can weigh up the considerations and make the final decision.

CHAPTER 2

Choosing the spot

Chapter 2Choosing the spot

Fantastic, you have settled on a rough area where you want to buy. Now, before you rush into your car and drive there and start annoying the estate agency offices, chill for a minute.

At this time, it is prudent to do some more background checks. Google the area, check for residents groups, Facebook pages, trip advisor reports, local authorities websites, do as much research as possible.

You are looking for anything out of the ordinary. There are some places which have a total ban on motor vehicles. Other areas are designated a preservation area which restricts any improvements you can make to a property and place strict guidelines on standard repairs like replacing windows and doors.

If you have had a thorough checkup and are satisfied, then stay with your computer and start researching property prices and estate agents who serve the area. This information will be invaluable when you go to look at properties. Never assume that prices are similar to where you currently live. I have known prices for a similar size home in rural areas to be only 20% of one's cost in a major city.

Make a shortlist of areas and properties which appeal to you, print out a map with all the properties marked to make it easier for you to go round them. Work out an efficient route between the properties to view them. Do not book viewings with the estate agent at this point. It is best to do a drive-by first, as very often, the property you see on the website is not the same as in the flesh. Half of your chosen properties may well be discarded at first glance.

OK, you have done all your homework. I know what it is like to be itching at the bit to get there and start physically inspecting and finding your dream property. Book some time off work, check how much funds are available to you and off you go. Make a holiday of it, if you have never been there before. It's not a good idea to buy, then discover later you do not like the place. Stay there, immerse yourself in it, and do not commit to buying until you know the area inside out.

Walk the area at different times of the day, especially around the properties you have identified as of interest. Is there plenty of parking available at all times? Some of these fishermen's cottages are very close together and on narrow streets not designed for motor cars. Indeed, this adds to the quaintness but comes with some problems.

As with buying any property, check out the neighbours. These cheaper properties and areas may attract undesirables or may have neighbours who have a much more relaxed village attitude to life.

Many fishermen's cottages are built with their gable end to the sea for protection against the weather. When they were constructed, there was no central heating and double glazing, so they were built with a concern for preserving heat rather than having a good view.

Do you have views? If this is a requirement, make sure that there are no plans to build anything else in front of you. What is your need for local shops, schools, health care, and other essential services, not only now but also for the next 20-30 years if you are long-term owners.

Finally, if you have pretty much settled on a specific property, look for the nearest cafe and go in for a coffee or snack. Strike up a conversation with the owner or other locals present. Be specific with them, tell them the exact property you are interested in and see their reaction.

Locals will know the property's history and usually will be candid with you if there are any problems. One thing to beware of in small villages, there are often family feuds and petty jealousies, which may lead the person you are talking with to give an exaggerated or even false report on the property.

Any problems highlighted should not be taken at face value but rather to be checked out. It could be that the owner of the home made a poor report on the cafe and there is bad blood between them.

On the other hand, the owner of the café may be a best friend and will not tell you anything wrong about the home. You must judge this for yourself.

CHAPTER 3

Doing your homework

Chapter 3Doing your homework

We are motoring now. You have looked at many homes but have finally got it down to your ideal property, and you are ready to press the buy button.

STOP!

There are unique problems with many fishermen's cottages, and we must stop and think about these particular things now.

1. Most fishermen's cottages were built without damp-proof courses, so you must pay particular attention to the location regarding the ground around it. Is any part of the property underground at floor level? This is a recipe for dampness coming through the external walls. It is not insurmountable, but the rooms adjoining the property's outer walls should be checked for moisture by a specialist. If there is moisture in the inner walls, they need to be stripped back to the moisture's height, the cavity behind cleaned out and re-instated. This operation can be costly and should be considered when calculating a buying price.

2. Are there other properties very close or even adjoining? In many of these small villages with a constricted property environment, special rules may apply or be contained within the title deeds. Other properties nearby may have access over your property for maintenance, or you may have access onto their ground. There may be shared land for tasks such as clothes drying or gardening. This area may be more than just shared, and it could well be communal, with responsibilities attached to usage. Be particularly interested in spaces between your property and the next house, especially if it is a tiny space, difficult to access. I have seen and heard of an all-out war over such areas, so make sure you have checked out who owns what all-around your property.

3. Check the extent of your property title. Is it a freehold or a feudal title? Freehold means that you own the property and the land it stands on, although you do not own any minerals under the ground. Feudal means that you own the property but not the land, for which you will be liable to pay an annual rent. The feudal title is not ideal, as it is often accompanied by onerous conditions when coming to sell. If you want this property, find out if it is possible to buy out the feudal title to freehold.

4. Finally, one particular problem often endured in these areas is the failure of the ancient drainage and sewer systems. A quick and easy check for this is to look at the roadway outside your potential home. Does the street show sign of many repairs? There will always be some repairs, as since these homes were built, there will have been gas added, electric updated, telephone wires added, amongst other upgrades. We are looking for too many signs of recent excavations. If there are signs of this, then try to research it further. You may ask for details in the local water and waste department.

CHAPTER 4

Buying your dream home

Chapter 4Buying your dream home

Buying your property will be similar to buying any other property. I urge you to use a local solicitor for the purchase, as they will have local knowledge your solicitor at home will not have. This is particularly important in these properties with special or unique title deeds.

There may be particular terms or conditions attached if you are using a mortgage to buy the property and also when you are buying property insurance. If you are having any problems with these, consult the local solicitor, who will inevitably have encountered this problem before.

It would be best if you were sure to have the property examined and checked out by a local preservation agent for the presence of woodworm or dry rot. If there is a problem, this agent will take care of it before you move in. It is common to have these properties treated for woodworm, which comes with a twenty-five-year guarantee. Again, you may wish to consider any costs when making an offer on the property.

Great, now you are owners of a seaside fisherman's cottage. The first step is to furnish it, and here you must also be very careful. Many of these older properties have irregular stairways, doors, and sloping roofs, which can cause problems when furnishing the home.

We decided we wanted a king-size bed in one of my properties. When it was delivered, the base was fine as it was in two halves, but try as we could, we could not get the flexible, bendy mattress up the stair, and it had to be installed in the downstairs bedroom.

I know of many properties with particular stairway problems where the owner will remove the upstairs windows to install large furniture items. Fortunately, standard sash and case windows are designed to have the windows removed fairly easily at a minimal cost in these properties.

Beware of creating any local problems when moving in. Make sure any removal men do not block roads or accesses. You do not want to get off to a bad start with the neighbours.

Reach out cautiously to neighbours. In days gone past, there would have been tight-knit communities that would help each other and any new owners. This is no longer the case, as you will find many of the properties will most likely be holiday homes. Today, it is not unknown for an entire street to be holiday homes with no permanent residents.

There will still be some older generation residents who will still live the old way and welcome you into their community, but you will have to search them out. Welcome everyone you see with a smile and cheery hello until you can figure out who the community's bedrock is. Wait until you are well established and have plenty of local knowledge before volunteering for any local committees. Some committees are closed circles, while others welcome new blood. You have to figure out which are which.

These older properties always need something done to them. There are always maintenance issues, but you deserve a rest now, so take a small break before you start, as you will always find the job is more significant than you thought, more complicated than expected, and none of the sizes are metric. You will get used to it in a few years, but it will be a pest at the start. Enjoy a break!

CHAPTER 5

Renovations

Chapter 5 Renovations

Another good reason for taking that break is that it gives you some time to make some local friends. This may not seem important to you, but if you strike gold and make an excellent local friend who has maintained his home for years, you will be able to get invaluable help and advice.

You will find that some local problems require unique products to be used for repairs and renovations. If you have never lived close to the sea before, you will be looking at a stiff learning curve. Seawater destroys ordinary materials in a way that rain or freshwater does not.

Any inside work in your home will mostly be the same as any home you have ever had before, except for always remembering that the property does not have a proper damp-proof course, so you must take measures to avoid dampness at all times. Any time you are stripping off any plasterboard, ensure that you clean out space behind the wall. Any debris left there will cause dampness.

It may be a good time to tell you never to shut off the heating when you are away from home. Most properties will deteriorate if left empty, but these old fishermen's properties without a damp-proof course will deteriorate at an alarming rate if left without heat.

Any renovations to the outside must keep the property in the same style as the original. An example of this is when replacing windows. If you have the old-style windows with four separate panes, then the new windows must be the same. Sometimes you can be more flexible at the back of the property if it is not visible from the street, but it is best to check with the local planning department first.

Take meticulous care if doing any work on the roof. Near the coast, you have the problem of driving saltwater during high winds. The saltwater will find an entry point through any even minute gaps. It is similar for walls and windows. Always complete them without cutting corners if you want to avoid any problems later.

If you are applying exterior paint, ensure you use the highest grade of exterior paint, as it will be required to last through a harsh winter.

Many of these properties have no garden, but if you are lucky enough to have one with a small garden, do not try to grow the same plants you would grow in your previous home. Only hardy plants will thrive in this environment, and even then, sometimes it is a struggle.

It is best to use local tradesmen to do any renovations you are not comfortable carrying out yourself. Local workers will know all the problems faced with these cottages and may well have worked on your home before. As usual, you must sift out real knowledgeable, hard-working guys from the wasters, but this is the same everywhere, so standard rules apply there. Ask for recommendations and referrals.

CHAPTER 6

Annual maintenance

Chapter 6Annual maintenance

You will quickly get into an annual routine and find that you need to do some things every year, which previously you only carried out every three or four years.

Painting external woodwork should only be required every two years if you use good paint. It is best if you do this in September. Many people will do this as soon as the sunny days come, but near the sea, water will have penetrated the wood all winter, and it is best if it gets the entire summer to dry properly before painting. Late August or early September is ideal, as later the weather is starting to deteriorate again.

If there is any stonework, slabs or lock block around the house, this will get quite grubby over the winter, so early summer is an excellent time to clean this. We do not advise using a power washer as this removes the sealed surface and lets the algae grow faster in the future. Our favourite method is to mix up some thick bleach with water, around ten parts water to one part bleach and scrub the area with a stiff brush. Leave it for one hour if possible, then wash off with fresh water. If you can leave it overnight without inconveniencing anyone, this is better.

If possible, you should check your roof and clean your gutters every year. Any deterioration in this area can be fast and cause a lot of damage if water penetrates. If you are not physically able to do this or do not have the ladders and other equipment required, hire a local handyman. There are usually decent handymen who work only on the type of problems you get with these properties. They will have many years of experience and have perhaps even worked on your home before. Ask your neighbours for recommendations.

Always check around the property for any debris build-up against the outer walls. Any debris against exterior walls will translate to dampness within the property. You must also ensure a clear water run-off route as any water lying will seep through the walls.

Particular attention should be paid to areas around flat roofs or dormer windows. Flashing in these areas are often the first place water will start to come through the roof.

CHAPTER 7

Long term maintenance

Chapter 7Long term maintenance

There will be some maintenance required on a very long term that is never necessary for a regular home. Perhaps every twenty years, the main job you will do is to completely strip back the lower part of your internal walls, clean out behind the wallboard, replace and make good.

This job may need to be done more regularly if you have sandstone walls. Sandstone tends to crumble more, and often you can hear a piece fall behind the wall. If this is left to build up, it will transfer the moisture from the external walls, and your wallboard will become damp.

Most of these homes are built with stone and pointed between by cement or lime. The pointing will deteriorate in time and have to be picked out and replaced. An alternative is to completely render the wall and paint it for a longer-term solution. However, this will completely alter the appearance of your home.

CHAPTER 8

Living with the neighbours

Chapter 8Living with the neighbours

It is a whole different ball game living in a 'Fishertown' or 'Seatown' area. The homes are very close together, and it is all too simple to get annoyed by the simplest little things. Many times you have to count to ten before you say anything, especially if you are having an off day

Parking is a premium in these tight locations, and you may find that the guy next door has been parking right in front of your window for the past 40 years. Another neighbour may not have wheelie bins and uses your ones. He has been doing this for ten years and may not take it well if someone who has been around for only ten minutes tells him he can't continue to do this.

Clothes drying lines are another issue. If you do not have your own garden space with your drying area, tread carefully. If there are communal clothes drying areas, you may only be expected to use them on certain days.

Check out areas between your home and the neighbours home. Sometimes these areas are communal. Other times they are owned by one property. It is also widespread for one neighbour to tell everyone it belongs to him when it is communal. If it belongs to you, think carefully before closing it off or excluding other people who may have used it for decades.

There will also be many 'right of ways' in these areas. Try to learn where they are so that you do not block any, but also so you can enjoy them.

These are only a few of the common examples of issues that may crop up. There are hundreds of other problems that may cause offence and are best avoided if possible.

In one village I stayed in, there were a brother and sister who had not spoken to each other for forty years, all over a two feet strip of land between their two homes, which both claimed as their own.

In general, the advice is to live with each other, help each other and try to get along as best you can. If you do not have the same accent as the locals, you may be classed as an 'incomer'. Please do not take this as an insult. Nothing is meant by it. It is simply a distinguishing feature to them.

I was termed as an 'incomer' in the village I stayed in for 25 years for my entire stay, and I grew up only 6 miles away. Small small towns are different, but if you try to fit in and not change their ways, you will soon be accepted as part of the community. If you try to change them, you will never be accepted.

One final word. Many small communities can be very religious. If this is the case, be careful what activities you carry out on a Sunday. They may treat it as a day of rest and be annoyed if you hang out washing, wash your car, do repairs or any similar duties.

CHAPTER 9

Helping out and integrating into the community

Chapter 9Helping out and integrating into the community

Always be willing to help others in the community, especially the elderly. There is no faster way into their good graces. Be careful, though, of trying to join any committees. These may have long-standing unspoken traditions and pecking orders with which you do not want to get involved.

If a particular work interests you, make it clear you are interested. If they want you to join a committee, you will be asked soon enough.

Living in a small rural community brings some challenges. Gone are the days of the small corner shop, and often these communities can be quite a distance from the nearest shop. This can be an excellent area to help out, and if you are going shopping, some of the elderly folks may be glad if you were to offer to get a few things for them.

You will find that people in these communities tend to share a lot. If you have a specific tool that your neighbour does not have, he will think nothing of asking to borrow it. You would also be expected to ask for anything you are lacking.

When returning anything you have borrowed or even something that they have volunteered to lend you as they see you struggle, be sure to return it with a small gift. It cannot be anything too valuable to offend them, but something simple like a packet of biscuits. Especially appreciated are things you have taken the time to make for them, such as home bakes or a homemade trinket.

Above all, observe closely how they relate to each other and how they interact and try to follow this model closely, only after you start to be accepted.

CHAPTER 10

Making improvements

Chapter 10Making improvements

Making improvements is a big issue in these areas. Number one, you have to contend with a planning department determined to retain the area's character as closely as possible.

Number two, you will have to satisfy any neighbours that you are not taking away anything they deem as belonging to them or the community, which may be something as simple as a view.

The residents in these areas can be pretty reserved and say nothing about your plans, but think plenty. If you have any outside changes to your home, be sure to mention them to your neighbours well in advance and gauge their reactions closely.

Any changes inside will not affect your neighbours but may still fall foul of the planning and preservation regulations. If you are in any doubt about this, talk to the planning department officials and even if they say it is OK, ask them if there is any other office you should consult. There may be another department, and they assume you will know about it.

There is not often room for extension of the property in these areas, but if there is and you are planning this, be sure to talk to your neighbours first and ensure they approve. Then speak to your solicitor to ensure there are no conditions on the land you want to build on. I have known extensions built in the past that have had to be demolished due to legal issues.

Remember, any extension should be in the same design as the original house and sympathetic to the area's character. In some situations, changes may have been made to your property before planners started tightening up on the area's character, which would not now be acceptable. Planners will often take this opportunity to force you to re-instate other appearances of the original property.

Examples of this are where a previous owner has made a big picturesque window that is not sympathetic to the area. It was approved at the time, and planners can do nothing about it, but when you submit new plans, they will make it a condition to re-instate the original type of windows.

This marks the end of the book, apart from the bonus chapter. If you have enjoyed this book, we would ask you to help us.

1. We would be grateful if you could leave a review of the book on Amazon. These reviews are the lifeblood of my business, and without them, I would have no new customers, and I could no longer write books.
2. I would welcome you to contact us through my author website at www.jamesgwhitelaw.com. I can assure you and I am a real person and do not use a pen name. I will answer any questions you have as soon as I am able.
3. Finally, let your friends know that you read my book and enjoyed it on your social media pages.

   Thanks for reading the book, and enjoy your bonus chapter.
4.

Bonus ChapterManaging your cottage as a rental home

Bonus ChapterManaging your cottage as a rental home

If you are not staying in the house permanently and want to cover your expenses, you may consider renting the property to tourists on a short-term rental basis.

At one point in my career, I ran a business managing over fifty rental homes, so this is an area with which I am familiar and can offer you advice. I may write another book on this subject in the future, but I will outline the essential information. If you feel this is something you would like to learn more about, let me know to consider the matter.

Since I worked in the industry, many new laws have been applied, and the market is still evolving. You should check with the local authority precisely what is required as this may have changed even since I wrote this book.

Most authorities now require you to hold a certificate from the tourist authorities, and the tourist authority will stipulate what is required. It should also be noted that the Scottish Government have plans to introduce new legislation on this during the next session of parliament. The general requirements are as follows:

1. An electrical report on the home is required annually
2. A gas report on the property is required annually
3. The house must be fitted with smoke detectors, a gas detector and a carbon monoxide detector.
4. The property must be signed with fire regulations and escape routes. It must also have minimum fire fighting equipment.

5. The dwelling must be equipped for the number of people it sleeps with enough plates, cutlery, cups, glasses, bedding, chairs, and much more.
6. There must be a 24-hour contact number in case of emergency, posted conspicuously in the home.
7. Different regions will also have additional requirements

Many extras are good practice to encourage guests to return. If you have storage space, leave some beach equipment for guest's use, this is always appreciated.

A BBQ is always a welcome extra, but guests may leave it dirty. Consider it, but it is not absolutely necessary.

If you are in an area where you regularly get rain, then umbrellas may be included. If you have a good view, be sure to leave a pair of binoculars.

The business aspect of renting out the home is a vast subject, and I can only touch it here. How you go about it will depend on how much you want to rent it out and the type of client you want to attract.

It is good to set up a website, preferably an interactive one. They are relatively easy to set up these days, but if you are not comfortable doing it for yourself, you can contact me, and I can recommend someone who can host a website for you for a mere £200 per year.

Your website should handle all admin aspects for you and be able to act as a mailing list for past guests with special offers and such once you have a client list built up.

To start with, you will need to advertise for guests. If you are in a popular area, you may be able to pick up excess guests from other owners during busy periods, but be careful to give them something small in return or return the compliment another time.

You can also join established websites like Airbnb or any of the many websites set up expressly for short-term rentals. Airbnb is quite reasonably priced, but other sites may take up to 20% commission on a booking.

Your long term aim must be to have your marketing and booking service in-house, but this will take time, and the only way to build it up is to spend money on advertising.

Feel free to contact me for any help you may need. If I can, I will help. You can contact me through my website at www.jamesgwhitelaw.com

CPSIA information can be obtained
at www.ICGtesting.com
Printed in the USA
BVHW071449190521
607713BV00001B/271